THE COMPLETE GUIDE TO INFUSING FOOD & BEER

50 INDULGENT & ROBUST RECIPES

CHARLOTE ISLA

TABLE OF CONTENTS

INTRODUCTION

Beers with its sweet, toasty, malty or nutty taste can add depth to dishes from Breakfast to Snacks, Desserts and Main dishes. . And don't worry about getting drunk – virtually all of the alcohol evaporates during the cooking process. These dishes will have your guests wondering what the secret ingredient is (and coming back for more!).

Different beers pair well with different foods, so it's important to learn the taste differences before you hit the kitchen. Beer can be divided into two main groups: ales and lagers. Ale, the original beer, is brewed in a way that results in fruity, earthy flavours. Lagers make use of more modern brewing systems to be lighter and drier. Each type of beer has a distinctly different flavour that pairs well with certain foods. Below, you'll find a breakdown of several common types and some recipes that use each one.

Wheat Beers

Wheat beers are pale, often unfiltered (thus cloudy), and have fruity, mellow, crisp-edged flavours, well-matched for salads and fish.

Pale Ale and Bitter

Its crispness cuts beautifully through rich, fatty meats like game. Pale ale is stronger, with more bracing carbonation, and goes well with everything from bread and cheese to fish and chips.

Porter

It's less toasty than stout and less bitter than pale ale, and it picks up the flavours in stews especially well.

Stout

Stout brings out the flavours in everything from shellfish to stews. Because of its distinct coffee and chocolate notes, it's also perfect for blending into rich desserts.

HOMEMADE BEERS

1. Banana beer

Yield: 35 glasses

Ingredient

- 5 Ripe bananas; mashed

- 5 Oranges; juice from

- 5 Lemons; juice from

- 5 cups Sugar Water

Mix together and freeze. Fill large glass ⅓ full (or more) with frozen mixture and add 7-Up, Sprite, Ginger ale, etc.

2. Alcatraz wheat beer

Yield: 1 Serving

Ingredient

- 3 pounds Dried wheat extract

- 2 pounds Wheat malt

- 1 pounds Barley malt

- 1 pounds Dried malt extract

- 2½ ounce Mt. Hood hops

- Wyeast Wheat beer yeast

Make a yeast starter two days beforehand. Mash the three pounds of malt a la Miller. Boil for one hour, adding 1-$\frac{1}{2}$ ounces hops at the start, $\frac{1}{2}$ ounce at 30 minutes, and $\frac{1}{2}$ ounce at 5 minutes. Cool and pitch yeast.

Ferment. Bottle. I primed half the batch (5 gal) with ⅓ cup corn sugar and the other half with $\frac{1}{2}$ cup clover honey. After two weeks, the beer was great. The beer primed with honey, however, was way too carbonated.

3. A & w root beer

Yield: 1 Serving

Ingredient

- $\frac{3}{4}$ cup Sugar

- $\frac{3}{4}$ cup Hot water

- 1 liter Cold seltzer water

- $\frac{1}{2}$ teaspoon Root beer concentrate

- $\frac{1}{8}$ teaspoon Root beer concentrate

Dissolve the sugar in the hot water. Add the root beer concentrate and let cool.

Combine the root beer mixture with the cold seltzer water, drink immediately or store in refrigerator in tightly covered container.

4. Garlic beer

Yield: 1 Serving

Ingredient

- ½ pounds Pale malt extract

- 4 large Bulbs garlic peeled and Cleaned

- 1 ounce Northern Brewer hops

- London Ale

Separate and peel the cloves from four entire bulbs of garlic and lightly score the surface of the garlic cloves to increase surface area during the boil.

Add the extract, half of the garlic, and ½ ounce of hops. Total boil of 60 minutes

After the boil, chill the wort and strain the cooled wort into a 6-½ gallon primary. After three days of vigorous ferment in 6½ gallon

5. California common beer

Yield: 1 Serving

Ingredient

- $3\frac{1}{8}$ pounds Superbrau Plain Light

- 3 pounds Briess Gold DME

- $\frac{1}{2}$ pounds Crystal malt -- crushed

- $\frac{1}{4}$ pounds Malted barley

- $1\frac{1}{2}$ ounce Northern brewer hops

- $\frac{1}{2}$ ounce Cascade hops -- last 5 min

- 1 pack Wyeast 2112 or 1 Amsterdam Lager

- 4 ounces Priming sugar

Put malted barley on cookie sheet in over at 350 degrees for 10 min. Remove and crush lightly with rolling pin. Put crushed grains in muslin bag, put into 1 gal of cold water and bring to a boil. Remove grains. Take pot off heat, add syrup & DME & stir until dissolved.

Put back on heat and add $1\frac{1}{2}$ ounces northern brewer hops and boil for 30-45 minutes. Add $\frac{1}{2}$ ounce cascade hops for the last 5 min of boil. Add to 4 gallons of cold water.

6. Six hour root beer

Yield: 1 Serving

Ingredient

- 2 cups Sugar
- 1 teaspoon Yeast
- 2 tablespoons Root beer extract

Put ingredients in a gallon jug with about a quart of very warm water. Stir until ingredients are well mixed.

Finish filling the jug with warm water. Let stand
six hours (just lay the lid on top, do not screw on).
At the end of the six hours, screw lid on and
refrigerate.

7. Maerzen beer

Yield: 54 Serving

Ingredient

- 4 pounds Pale malt

- 3 pounds Light dry extract

- $\frac{1}{2}$ pounds Crystal malt (40L)

- 2 ounces Chocolate malt

- $\frac{1}{2}$ pounds Toasted malt

- $\frac{1}{2}$ pounds Munich malt

- 2 ounces Dextrin malt

- $2\frac{1}{2}$ ounce Tettnanger hops (4.2 alpha)

- $\frac{1}{2}$ ounce Cascade hops (5.0 alpha)

- 3 teaspoons   Gypsum

- Vierka dry lager yeast

Make up yeast starter 2 days before

Add 8 pints of boiling water and heat to 154 degrees. Set for at least 30 minutes. Bring to 170 degrees for 5 minutes for mash out. Sparge with 2 gallons water. Add dry extract, bring to boil. Boil 15 minutes and add one ounce of Tettnanger. Boil one hour. Add 1 ounce of Tettnanger at 30 minutes. Add $\frac{1}{2}$ ounce of Tettnanger and $\frac{1}{2}$ ounce of Cascade at 5 minutes. Strain and chill.

8. Cottage beer

Yield: 1 Serving

Ingredient

- 1 Peck good wheat bran

- 3 Handful hops

- 2 quarts Molasses

- 2 tablespoons Yeast

- 10 gallons Water

Put bran and hops into water, and boil until bran
and hops sink to the bottom. Strain through a thin
cloth into a cooler.

When it is about lukewarm, add molasses. As soon as molasses is dissolved, pour all into a 10-gallon cask and add yeast.

When fermentation is over with, cork up the cask and it will be ready in 4-5 days.

9. Cranberry beer

Yield: 1 Serving

Ingredient

- 6 pounds Extra light dry malt Extract

- 1 pounds Munich malt

- 1 ounce Fuggles boiling

- 3 Bags frozen cranberries

- 1 ounce Fuggles as finishing hops

- Yeast

Thaw the berries and blend with enough water to make a little over 2 quarts of slush.

Meanwhile, do a normal extract brew using the Munich malt as a specialty grain.

At the end of the hour of boiling, put in the finishing hops and poured in the cranberry liquid for the final minute or two as you turn off the heat.

Bottle after a week

10. Ginger beer cordial

Yield: 1 Serving

Ingredient

- 2 ounces Root Ginger, Peeled and chopped

- 1 pounds Granulated Sugar

- $\frac{1}{2}$ ounce Tartaric Acid

- Juice of 1 lemon

- 1 Lemon, Sliced

Put the ginger, sugar, tartaric acid and lemon into a bowl and cover with 1 gallon of boiling water. Stir until the sugar has dissolved.

Leave for about three or four days, then strain and pour the liquid into sterilized bottles. It will be ready and really delicious to drink after just a few days and can be diluted quite happily with either still or sparkling water.

11. Tomato beer cooler

Yield: 6 Serving

Ingredient

- 1½ cups tomato juice, chilled

- 2 cans (12 oz each) beer

Garnish:

- green onions

- red pepper sauce

- salt and pepper

Mix 1½ cups tomato juice, chilled and 2 cans (12 oz each) beer, chilled. Pour into chilled glasses. Serve immediately with green onions for stirrers and, if desired, with red pepper sauce, salt and pepper.

BEER COCKTAILS

12. Beer margarita

Yield: 1 Serving

Ingredient

- 6 ounce Can frozen concentrated Limeade

- 6 ounce Tequila

- 6 ounce Beer

Combine ingredients in blender, add a couple of ice cubes and blend briefly. Allow to set for a few minutes.

Pour contents over ice in salt rimmed glass.

13. Classic Chelada

Ingredients

- 12 ounce Mexican lager beer

- 1 ounce (2 tablespoons) lime juice

- 1 pinch salt

- Ice, for serving (try clear ice)

- For the rim: 1 tablespoon each fine sea salt and Old Bay

Instructions

On a plate, mix the Old Bay and salt and spread it into an even layer. Cut a notch in a lime wedge, and then run the lime around the rim of a glass. Dip the edge of the rim into a plate of salt.

Add the lime juice and pinch of salt to the beer glass. Fill the glass with ice and pour in the beer. Stir gently and serve.

14. Michelada

Ingredients

- 12-ounce Mexican lager beer

- 1 ½ ounces (3 tablespoons) lime juice

- ½ ounce (1 tablespoon) salsa juice

- 1 teaspoon Worcestershire sauce

- 1 teaspoon hot sauce (like Cholula)

- Ice, for serving

Instructions

On a plate, mix the Old Bay, chili powder and celery salt and spread it into an even layer. Cut a notch in a lime wedge, and then run the lime around the rim of a glass. Dip the edge of the rim into a plate of seasonings.

In the glass, stir together the lime juice, salsa juice (use a fine-mesh strainer to strain out salsa juice from a few spoonfuls of salsa), Worcestershire sauce, and hot sauce.

Fill the glass with ice. Top with the beer and stir gently.

15. Black Velvet Drink

Ingredients

- 3 ounces sparkling wine, like champagne or Prosecco

- 3 ounces stout beer, like Guinness

Instructions

Pour the sparkling wine into a flute or highball.

Pour in the stout. Stir with a bar spoon if desired, or allow to sit for a minute or so to allow flavors to marry

Serve immediately.

16. Classic Shandy

Ingredients

- 6 ounces pale ale or lager beer

- 6 ounces ginger ale, ginger beer, lemon lime soda (Sprite), or sparkling lemonade

- For the garnish: lemon wedge (optional)

- Optional: 1 dash bitters adds a complex flavor

Instructions

Add the beer and mixer to a glass and stir gently to combine. Garnish with a lemon wedge.

17. Grapefruit Shandy

Ingredients

- 1 ounce simple syrup

- 3 ounces grapefruit juice

- 2 ounces soda water

- 6 ounces craft wheat beer (or light beer)

- For the garnish: grapefruit wedge (optional)

Instructions

In a beer glass, stir the simple syrup and grapefruit juice.

Add the soda water and beer and stir gently to combine. Garnish with a grapefruit wedge and serve.

18. Strawberry Cucumber Spritzer

Ingredients:

- 6 oz Stella Artois Spritzer
- 1 oz gin
- .5 oz elderflower liqueur
- 2 cucumber slices
- 2 strawberries

Directions:

In a cocktail shaker, muddle cucumber slices and strawberries thoroughly. Add gin, elderflower liqueur, and shake over ice.

Strain into a glass. Add Stella Artois Spritzer.

Garnish with skewered cucumber ribbon and strawberry slice.

19. Beergarita

Ingredients:

- 1 oz. Tequila

- 1 oz. Tattersall Grapefruit Crema

- .5 oz. Lime Juice

- 6 oz. Light beer

Directions:

Combine all ingredients in a glass over ice. Garnish with a lime wedge.

Salt rim optional

20. Bacardi Lime Shot with Beer

Ingredients:

- 12 parts Beer

- 1 part Bacardi Lime

Directions:

Pour beer in a glass. Pour BACARDÍ Lime flavored rum in a shot glass and then pour into the beer.

21. Fidelito

Ingredients:

- 12 oz. Modelo Negra
- 1 ½ oz. Casa Noble Reposado Tequila
- ½ oz. PIMM'S THE ORIGINAL No. 1 Cup
- 1 oz. lime juice
- 1 oz. vanilla syrup
- 2 dashes bitters
- Mint leaves

Directions:

Mix all ingredients in a shaker with ice, excluding Modelo Negra and mint leaves.

Shake and pour over ice. Top with Modelo Negra.

Serve remaining beer with cocktail. Garnish with mint leaves.

22. Beermosa

Ingredients:

- 6 oz Wheat Beer
- 2 oz Cava
- 2 oz fresh squeeze grapefruit juice

Directions:

Mix the beer and cava, insert grapefruit juice and mix.

23. Sunshine Boilermaker

Ingredients:

- 1 can of pale lager
- 1.5 oz. of bourbon
- Sparkling Ice Lemon Lime
- Lemon (garnish)

Directions:

In a pint glass, pour beer at an angle to eliminate head. Add 1.5 oz. of bourbon. Top with Sparkling Ice Lemon Lime. Garnish with lemon wedge.

24. Cinco

Ingredients:

- 12 oz. Modelo Negra
- 1 oz. jalapeno-infused reposado tequila
- 1 oz. Chile liqueur
- 1 oz. fresh lime juice
- ½ oz. agave
- Spicy chili salt
- Lime wheel

Directions:

Rim a highball glass with spicy chili salt. Add tequila, Chile liqueur, fresh lime and agave to a shaker.

Shake and strain over fresh ice. Top off with beer. Serve remaining Modelo Negra with the cocktail.

Garnish with spicy chili salt rim and lime wheel.

DESSERTS

25. Beer and sauerkraut fudge

Yield: 10 Serving

Ingredient

- ⅔ cup Butter

- 1½ cup Sugar

- 3 Eggs

- 1 teaspoon Vanilla

- ½ cup Cocoa

- 2¼ cup Sifted flour

- 1 teaspoon Baking powder

- 1 teaspoon Soda

- 1 cup Beer

- ⅔ cup Sauerkraut

- 1 cup Raisins

- 1 cup Chopped nuts

Blend everything.

Turn into two 8 or 9 inch greased and floured cake pans. Bake at 350 for 35 minutes. Cool and frost as desired.

26. Beer biscuits

Yield: 4 Serving

Ingredient

- 2 cups Unbleached Flour

- 3 teaspoons Baking Powder

- 1 teaspoon Salt

- $\frac{1}{4}$ cup Shortening

- $\frac{3}{4}$ cup Beer

Preheat Oven to 450 degrees F. Sift dry ingredients together. Cut in shortening until it has cornmeal consistency.

Stir in beer, knead lightly, and roll out to ½-inch thickness. Bake 10 - 12 minutes or until golden brown.

27. Spice beer cake

Yield: 12 Serving

Ingredient

- 3 cups Flour
- 2 teaspoons Baking soda
- ½ teaspoon Salt
- 1 teaspoon Cinnamon
- ½ teaspoon Allspice
- ½ teaspoon Cloves
- 2 cups Brown sugar, packed

- 2 Eggs, beaten

- 1 cup Shortening

- 1 cup Raisins or chopped dates

- 1 cup Chopped pecans/walnuts

- 2 cups Beer

Sift together dry ingredients. Cream together shortening and sugar; add eggs.

Mix fruit and nuts with 2 tablespoons of the flour mixture. Add flour mixture alternately with beer. Stir in fruit and nuts.

Pour into a greased and floured 10-in tube pan and bake at 350F for 1 hour, or until cake tests done.

28. Beer cheese soup with popcorn

Yield: 7 Serving

Ingredient

- $\frac{1}{4}$ cup Margarine

- 1 cup Onion; chopped

- $\frac{1}{2}$ cup Celery; chopped

- $\frac{1}{2}$ cup Carrot; chopped

- $\frac{1}{4}$ cup Fresh parsley; chopped

- 2 Cloves garlic; minced

- $\frac{1}{4}$ cup Flour

- 3 teaspoons Dry mustard

- Pepper to taste

- 2 cups Half and half

- 1 cup Chicken broth

- 2$\frac{1}{2}$ cup American cheese

- 12 ounces Beer

- 2 cups Popcorn; popped

Melt margarine in a large saucepan or Dutch oven over medium heat.Add everything

Cook uncovered over medium heat 10-15 minutes or until soup is thickened and thoroughly heated

29. Stuffed apples baked in beer

Yield: 6 Serving

Ingredient

- 6 mediums Cooking apples
- $\frac{1}{2}$ cup Raisins
- $\frac{1}{2}$ cup Packed brown sugar
- 1 teaspoon Cinnamon
- 1 cup Great Western Beer

Core apples

Remove 1-inch strip of peel around top.

Mix raisins, brown sugar and cinnamon. Fill apple centers

Place apples in a baking dish. Pour Great Western Beer over.

Bake at 350 degrees F for 40 to 45 min, or until tender, basting occasionally.

30. Cheddar & beer cheesecake

Yield: 16 Serving

Ingredient

- 1¼ cup Gingersnap cookie crumbs

- 1 cup Plus 2 tablespoons sugar, divided

- 1 teaspoon Ground ginger

- ¼ cup Unsalted butter or margarine,

- 24 ounces Cream cheese

- 1 cup Shredded sharp Cheddar cheese

- 5 large Eggs, at room temperature

- ¼ cup Non-alcoholic beer

- ¼ cup Heavy cream

Combine the cookie crumbs, 2 tablespoons of the sugar, the ginger, and butter. Press firmly into the bottom of the prepared pan. Chill while making the filling.

Beat both cheeses just until smooth. Add sugar, eggs, one at a time, beating just until each is combined. At low speed, beat in the beer and heavy cream. Pour into the prepared pan.

Bake for 1½ hours or until the center is set and the top is lightly golden, but do not brown.

31. British fruit beer

Yield: 1 Serving

Ingredient

- 3⅓ pounds Amber plain malt

- 2 pounds M&F amber beer

- 1 pounds Crustal malt, crushed

- 2 ounces Northern brewer hops

- 1 ounce   Fuggles hops

- 4 pounds Blueberries, raspberries or

- 1 pack EDME ale yeast

- 4 ounces Priming sugar

Put crushed grains in muslin bag & place in 1 gal of cold water. Bring to boil, remove grains.

Remove pot from heat and add syrup & DME. Stir until dissolved. Return pot to heat & add 2 oz northern brewer hops. Boil for 30-45 minutes. Add the figgles hops for the last 5 min of boil. Add fruit to wort when the boiling is finished.

Steep for ½ hour and add 4 gal of cold water.

32. Basic beer bread

Yield: 1 Serving

Ingredient

- 3 cups Flour

- $3\frac{3}{4}$ teaspoon Baking powder

- $2\frac{1}{4}$ teaspoon Salt

- 1 can Beer

- 1 tablespoon Honey

Grease loaf pan. Combine flour, baking powder, salt, beer, and honey in large bowl, stir together until well mixed.

Bake in preheated 350 F oven for 45 minutes. Turn on rack and cool.

33. Cheesy beer muffins

Yield: 6 Serving

Ingredient

- 1 cup All-Purpose Flour

- ¾ cup Low-fat Cheddar Cheese

- 4 teaspoons Sugar

- 1¼ teaspoon Baking Powder

- ¼ teaspoon Baking Soda

- ¼ teaspoon Salt

- ⅔ cup Beer

- 1 Egg, Beaten

Heat oven to 375F

Spray 6 muffin cups with nonstick cooking spray.

Lightly spoon flour into measuring cup; level off. In med bowl, combine flour, cheese, sugar, baking powder, baking soda and salt; mix well. Add beer and egg; stir just until dry ingredients are moistened. Divide batter evenly into sprayed muffin cups, filling each about ¾ full.

Bake at 375F for 17 - 22 min or until golden brown and toothpick inserted in center comes out clean. Serve warm or at room temp.

34. Dill beer bread

Yield: 12 Serving

Ingredient

- 3 cups Flour

- 1 tablespoon Sugar

- 1½ tablespoon Baking powder

- ¼ teaspoon Salt

- 12 ounces Beer

- 3 tablespoons Fresh dill

Preheat the oven to 375 degrees. Butter a loaf pan, or spray with vegetable oil spray. Sift the flour, sugar, baking powder and salt into a mixing bowl. Stir in the beer and dill. Scrape the batter into the prepared loaf pan and bake in the center of the oven for 55 to 60 minutes, or until brown on top and knife inserted into the center comes out clean.

Allow to sit in the pan 10 minutes, and then cool on a rack.

SNACKS

35. Beer nuts

Yield: 1 Serving

Ingredient

- 2 cups Raw Peanuts (skins on)

- 1 cup SUGAR

- ½ cup WATER

- Few drops of RED food coloring

Mix - Cook in heavy pan over med heat till water is gone (about 10-15 min) Spread on Baking Sheet Bake 1 hour at 250

36. Fried asparagus in beer batter

Yield: 1 Serving

Ingredient

- 1 each To 2 pounds asparagus

- 1 cup Flour

- 1 can Beer

- Salt and pepper

- Garlic powder

- Seasoned salt

- Italian seasoning, to taste

- Olive oil

Mix flower and seasonings together. Add beer to fry ingredients mixing slowly until thick enough to cling to asparagus. Cut asparagus into two inch pieces or leave whole.

Deep fry in two inches olive oil until golden brown, turning once

37. Orange spritz cookies

Yield: 1 Serving

Ingredient

- 2¼ cup Flour

- 1 tablespoon Baking powder

- ¼ teaspoon Salt

- ¾ cup Butter

- ½ cup Sugar

- 1 Egg

- 2 teaspoons Grated orange peel

- $\frac{1}{2}$ teaspoon Almond extract

Combine flour, baking powder and salt; set aside.

Cream butter and sugar until light and fluffy, beat in egg, orange peel and almond extract

Add dry ingredients and beat until combined.

Don not chill the dough.

Pack dough into cookie press. Force dough through press onto an ungreased baking sheet. If desired decorate with colored sugar or candies.

Bake at 400~ for 6-8 minutes. Remove to wire racks to cool.

38. Beer griddlecakes

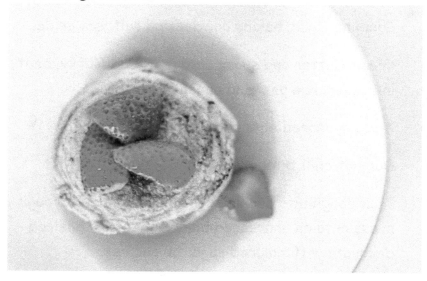

Yield: 4 Serving

Ingredient

- 1¾ cup All-purpose flour
- 1½ teaspoon Baking powder
- ½ teaspoon Baking soda
- ½ teaspoon Salt
- 1 cup Packed brown sugar
- ½ cup Beer
- 1 Egg

- 3 tablespoons Oil

- 1 tablespoon Molasses

- 1 Bottle beer

- 1 tablespoon Butter (optional)

Mix dry ingredients. Beat egg with oil and molasses. Add to dry ingredients along with beer.

Spoon batter onto hot and very lightly greased griddle

Spread with back of spoon to $3\frac{1}{2}$ to 4 inches in diameter. Cook until browned, turning once.

For syrup, combine ingredients in saucepan and boil for minutes.

39. Smokies in beer and honey

Yield: 6 Serving

Ingredient

- 1 pounds Miniature smokie-links

- 12 ounces Beer

- ½ cup Honey

Brown smokies in pan big enough to hold all ingredients

Pour beer and honey over smokies and bring to boil. Reduce heat and cover.

Simmer for 15 minutes. Transfer to serving dish and stand back out of the way.

40. Beer batter onion rings

Yield: 2 Serving

Ingredient

- 1⅓ cup All-purpose flour

- 1 teaspoon Salt

- ¼ teaspoon Pepper

- 1 tablespoon Oil

- 2 Egg yolks

- ¾ cup Beer

- 2 large White onions sliced 1/4-in thick

- Oil for deep frying

Mix the flour, salt, pepper, oil and yolks together. Gradually whisk in the beer. Refrigerate the batter $3\frac{1}{2}$ hours to rest before using.

Slice onions, and dip them in the batter. Deep-fry in 375F oil until golden brown. This batter also works well on other vegetables besides onion rings--and it's great on fish, too.

41. Cheese & beer dip

Yield: 1 Serving

Ingredient

- 1 cup Cottage cheese; small curd
- 3 ounce Cream cheese
- $2\frac{1}{4}$ ounce Deviled ham
- $\frac{1}{4}$ cup Beer; New Glarus Solstice
- $\frac{1}{2}$ teaspoon Hot sauce
- 1 dash Salt
- Parsley; for garnish

Put all ingredients except parsley into a mixing bowl and beat until smooth. Place in bowl and garnish with parsley

42. Tempura beer batter

Yield: 1 Serving

Ingredient

- 1¼ cup   Flour

- 1 teaspoon Salt

- 1 teaspoon Finely ground black pepper

- ½ teaspoon Cayenne

- 1 12-ounce lager beer; (cold)

- Veg oil for deep frying; (360 deg. F.)

Whisk quickly; don't over Mix! Leave Lumps & use batter immediately.

43. German Barbecue sauce

Yield: 12 Serving

Ingredient

- 2 Bottles (14-oz) catsup

- 1 Bottle (12-oz) chili sauce

- ½ cup Prepared mustard

- 1 teaspoon Dry mustard

- 1 teaspoon Salt

- 1½ cup   Brown sugar; firmly packed

- 2 tablespoons Black pepper

- 1 Bottle (5-oz) steak sauce

- ½ cup Worcestershire sauce

- 1 tablespoon Soy sauce

- 1 Bottle (12-oz) beer

- 2 teaspoons Mince garlic

Combine all ingredients, except garlic, in saucepan and simmer 30 minutes over medium heat. Add minced garlic before using.

Baste meat during last 15 minutes of grilling time.

44. Basic beer mop

Yield: 3 Serving

Ingredient

- 12 ounces Beer
- ½ cup Cider Vinegar
- ½ cup Water
- ¼ cup Canola Oil
- ½ medium Onion, chopped
- 2 Cloves Garlic Clove, Minced

- 1 tablespoon Worcestershire Sauce

- 1 tablespoon Dry Rub

Combine all ingredients in a saucepan. Heat the mop and use it warm.

45. Beer batter for fish

Yield: 6 Serving

Ingredient

- 1 cup All-Purpose Flour
- $\frac{3}{4}$ teaspoon Baking powder
- $\frac{1}{2}$ teaspoon Salt
- $\frac{1}{2}$ cup Water
- $\frac{1}{2}$ cup Beer
- 1 each Egg
- Vegetable Oil for deep frying

- 2 pounds Fish Fillets

One of the best batter recipes going

In bowl, stir together flour, baking powder and salt. Make a well in the center; pour in water, beer and egg, whisking to make a smooth batter. Let stand 20 minutes.

Heat oil in large saucepan to 350F

Dip fish fillets in batter, adding to hot oil one at a time. Cook about 5 minutes, turning once or twice, until golden and crisp. Remove to paper towel-lined plate.

46. Beer and edam spread

Yield: 3 cups

Ingredient

- 2 7-oz rounds Edam cheese

- 8 ounces Carton dairy sour cream

- $\frac{1}{4}$ cup Beer

- 2 teaspoons Snipped chives

- Snipped chives

- Assorted crackers

Bring cheese to room temperature. Cut a circle from the top of each cheese round, about $\frac{1}{2}$ inch from edge. Remove the cut circle of paraffin coating

Carefully scoop cheese out, leaving $\frac{1}{2}$ inch of cheese intact to form a shell

Place sour cream, beer, chives, and cheese in a blender container or food processor bowl. Cover and process till smooth, stopping machine occasionally to scrape down sides.

Spoon cheese mixture into shells

Cover and chill several hours or overnight.

Garnish with chives, if desired. Serve with crackers.

47. Cheese and chili beer dip

Yield: 1 Serving

Ingredient

- 2 cups Grated sharp Cheddar

- $\frac{3}{4}$ cup Beer (not dark)

- 2 cups Grated Jarlsberg

- $\frac{1}{2}$ cup Drained canned tomatoes

- 2 tablespoons All-purpose flour

- 1 Bottle pickled jalapeno chili, minced

- 1 small Onion; minced

- Tortilla chips as an accompaniment

- 1 tablespoon Unsalted butter

In a bowl toss the cheeses with the flour and reserve the mixture.

In a large heavy saucepan cook the onion in the butter over moderately low heat, stirring, until it is softened, add the beer, the tomatoes, and the jalapeño, and simmer the mixture for 5 minutes.

Add the reserved cheese mixture by $\frac{1}{2}$ cupful's to the beer mixture, stirring after each addition until the cheeses are melted, serve the dip with the chips. Makes $4\frac{1}{2}$ cups

48. Beer fish sauce

Yield: 1 Serving

Ingredient

- 1 cup Mayonnaise

- ¼ cup Catsup

- ¼ cup Beer

- 1 tablespoon Prepared mustard

- 1 tablespoon Lemon juice

- 1 teaspoon Prepared horseradish

Combine all ingredients.

Chill and serve with fish.

49. Beer marinade for beef

Yield: 8 Serving

Ingredient

- 2 cans Beer (12 oz or 10 oz cans)

- 2 teaspoons Salt

- ½ cup Olive oil

- 1 teaspoon Ground cayenne pepper

- 1 tablespoon Wine vinegar

- 1 tablespoon Prepared horseradish

- 1 teaspoon Onion powder

- 2 tablespoons Lemon juice

- 1 teaspoon Garlic powder

Mix all ingredients together and use as a marinade.

Then use as a basting sauce for the meat whiles it cooks.

50. Mexican beer salsa

Yield: 4 Serving

Ingredient

- 4 each Dried ancho chiles

- 6 large Ripe tomatoes

- $\frac{3}{4}$ cup Diced white onions

- 4 each Cloves garlic

- 1 tablespoon Coarse salt

- $\frac{1}{2}$ teaspoon Black pepper

- $\frac{1}{2}$ cup Mexican beer

- ½ cup Chopped cilantro leaves

Preheat oven to 400 degrees. Soak anchos in hot water until soft, about 10 to 15 minutes. Drain water and stem and seed chiles. (Use gloves.) Place tomatoes, onion, garlic, and chiles in a roasting pan and roast in oven for 20 minutes until skins of tomatoes char.

Remove and place all in blender or food processor and pulse briefly until pureed but still chunky. Pour into saucepan and bring to a simmer. Stir in salt, pepper and beer. Remove from heat and add cilantro. Serve warm. Makes 4 cups

CONCLUSION

The merits of Cooking and infusing with beer extend way beyond cracking open a cold one after a long day. Brews of all shades can be used in cooking too...

Its very much worth taking the time and effort to match beer with food. The same principle applies when using wine to add body and flavour to dishes, and beer is (usually) cheaper than vino. As beer is so complex, you should use different shades and styles for appropriate recipes, and this book has equipped you with a ideas to get started!

Lightning Source UK Ltd.
Milton Keynes UK
UKHW020745250621
386136UK00005B/82